A Jungian Approach To
BIPOLAR DISORDER
Rejoining The Split Archetype

By Jason Thompson

Contents

"It is not a matter if indifference whether one calls something a 'mania' or a 'god'. To serve a mania is detestable and undignified, but to serve a god is full of meaning."
C.G. Jung

Jung on Manic-Depression

Descriptions of manic and depressive states have been recorded throughout written history. However it was not until 1899 that the brilliant German psychiatrist Emil Kraeplin provided the first reliable conceptualisation of manic-depressive illness as a disease having an undulating course rather than an irreversible downhill slide as in chronic psychosis. A mere four years later while working at the Burgholzli Psychiatric Hospital in Zurich, a young Carl Jung wrote his landmark paper On Manic mood Disorder (1903).

What was noteworthy about Jung's essay is that it was the first to call for a diagnostic distinction to be made between manic-depression involving psychotic states, and that which does not involve psychosis. Jung's distinction is today referred to in the DSM-V as that between 'bipolar I' (involving psychotic episodes) and 'bipolar II' (without psychosis). In this paper Jung introduces the non-psychotic version of the illness with the introductory statement, "I would like to publish a number of cases whose peculiarity consists in chronic hypomanic behaviour" where "it is not a question of real mania at all but of a hypomanic state which cannot be regarded as psychotic" (Jung 1903). Jung fills out this proposition with 5 case histories, each involving hypomanic behaviour, occasional bouts of depression, and mixed mood states, which involved personal and interpersonal upheaval for each patient. Of particular interest he provides 12 separate descriptions of what psychiatry today refers to as 'mixed mood states'.

Mixed Mood States

In the context of psychiatric disorders a mixed mood state (also known as dysphoric mania, agitated depression, or simply a mixed episode) is a condition during which symptoms of mania and depression occur simultaneously (e.g., mixtures of agitation, anxiety, fatigue, guilt, impulsiveness, irritability, morbid or suicidal ideation, panic, paranoia, pressured speech and rage). Typical examples include tearfulness during a manic episode or racing thoughts during a depressive episode. One may also feel incredibly frustrated or be prone to fits of rage in this state, since one may feel like a failure and at the same time have a flight of ideas. Mixed states are often the most dangerous period of mood disorders, during which susceptibility to substance abuse, panic disorder, commission of violence, suicide attempts, and other complications increase greatly. Jung provides clear descriptions of mixed states in the following accounts;

> 'On admission the patient was slightly inebriated, euphoric, very talkative, showing a flight of ideas. Told that his mother would visit him the next day, he got excited, wept, [and] declared he was not in a fit state to receive her.' (p.113)

'She was extremely labile, at one moment
with tears in her eyes, shouting with laughter
the next, up to all sorts of tricks.' (p.116)

'She was very elated, very erotic, flirting and
laughing a great deal; very labile, weeping
easily at the memory of unhappy experiences;
liked to sulk ostentatiously, and once made a
violent scene when the doctor refused to visit
her alone in her room, threatened suicide, so
that she had to be removed for a while to the
observation room.' (p.123)

'His behaviour varied as before; mostly he
was elated and excited, bit intermittently he
was irritable, with stormy moods.' (p.128)

Aside from his observations regarding hypomania and
mixed states, Jung makes reference to episodes of
ultra-rapid cycling between mania and depression, a
little understood or recognised phenomenon at the
time of his writing. He provides further accounts of
individuals regulating moods with chronic
alcoholism, binge eating and impulsiveness, the finer
details of which I will leave for the interested reader
to follow up in his paper.

With Jung's essay providing rich case material and
setting the scene for potential further investigation
into bipolar disorder it seems remarkable that almost
no later writers (including Jungians) refer to it. There
have appeared just two short essays on manic
depression from a Jungian perspective, that I am

aware of, in the 100 years since Jung's paper was written.

The purpose of this essay then is to survey the available material from Jung (given above) and post Jungians contributions (below), and finally to add some observations on the puer-senex archetype as archetypal basis of the bipolar disorder, with particular reference to James Hillman's description of this archetypal phenomenon.

Jole Cappiello McCurdy

The first of the post-Jung essays to appear was Jole Cappiello McCurdy's (1987) *'Manic-Depressive Psychosis – A Perspective: Binswanger, Jung, Neumann, and the Myth of Dionysus.'* McCurdy begins by acknowledging Jung's 1903 paper, while making the odd complaint that Jung has "left us neither a unitary description of the psychosis nor an interpretation of it" adding, "It is the purpose of this paper, therefore, to formulate a Jungian hypothesis of manic-depressive illness."

McCurdy's point that Jung did not give a "description of the psychosis" is moot, as Jung set out to define a common mood disorder characterized precisely *by the absence of psychosis*. McCurdy is right however in saying that Jung did not provide a universal unitary description of manic depressive illness (and all variants), nor substantive interpretations.

To be fair to Jung we should note that his stated aim was to provide a phenomenology of non-psychotic manic-depressive disorder, and in this he succeeded admirably. The paper is a remarkably rich detailed exploration for the time in which it was written.

McCurdy's paper is dense with linkages between ideas of Jung, Binswanger, Neumann, and the myth of Dionysus. Her thesis is that the disorder is at root *not affective*, but rather a dysfunction in the ego's relationship with a principle of unification –the Self. Following the lead of Erich Neumann, McCurdy suggests that the dysfunctional ego-self dynamic takes root in the primal relationship where the mother is unable to mediate the unifying function of the Self to the child's emergent ego, leaving the latter subject to wild oscillations of imagery and resultant mood:

> '[This] pathological development is possible if the ego becomes split off from its connecting axis with the self. In this situation the ego retains its essential identity, but, being more or less cut off from the self, manifests the accentuated rootlessness reminiscent of conditions found in the phenomenology of manic-depressive psychotic states. In these cases there is a loss of true orderedness of the world, with its rules of temporal sequence and natural cause and effect. Moreover, we can hypothesise that the transcendent function, as an expression of the connection between the unconscious and the conscious, between the self and the ego, is paralysed or blocked. Therefore, in manic-depressive states, the ability to form symbols is lost, with the result that life, instead of following a natural flow,

becomes, in Binswanger's terms, extremely problematic.

The antinomy melancholia-mania can be seen, therefore, as the expression of the rupture of the ego/self axis. As a consequence of the rupture, the self cannot actualise itself through the ego: it cannot fulfil its directive function or produce symbols or a synthesis through human consciousness. The ego remains suspended between two opposites of the totality, between its dark and luminous sides, oscillating between the two poles of depression and elation.

Binswanger theorised that the apparent polar conditions of manic and depressive disorders derived from the same basic inability of the ego to order and give meaning to experience. Although the pure ego is still capable of self-identity, it is, however, paralysed in its directive function because the transcendental ego, with its category of time, is dysfunctional. From a Jungian point of view, I suggest further that the ego's defect derives from a severely damaged ego/self axis, an expression of a failure of the primal relationship.' (McCurdy, p.230)

McCurdy claims to find the disordered ego-Self dynamic portrayed in the biography and behaviour of the god Dionysus who "enacts an archetypal version of the failed primal relationship, with the resultant swings between the opposites and inability to find a centre" (p.323).

The remedy for Dionysus' condition, claims McCurdy, comes in the form of women who can impart a uniting, mediating function of the Self. Thus Dionysus' obsession with women, with mothers and nurses, can be seen as "a frantic attempt to repair the break, to experience the primal relationship he never had" (p.322).

The mythical figure of Ariadne symbolises another possible successful resolution to the fate of Dionysus. Ariadne, who bears the shining crown and connecting thread, personifies the ego-Self axis and relationship among the different realms of the psyche; this according to McCurdy represents the very real possibilities of transformation and the synthesis of opposites so urgently needed in the oscillating movement of manic-depression.

Having outlined McCurdy's view of manic-depression as based in the archetypes of ego and Self, we can move on to my own view of the condition as indeed involving lack of synthesis between opposites (per McCurdy), but involving a completely different pair of archetypes than that offered by McCurdy - specifically the archetypes of *puer* and *senex*, a view finding agreement in the second of the post-Jung writers on manic-depression I intend to survey below, the Italian psychoanalyst and Jungian Luigi Zoja.

Before quoting Zoja let me give a brief comment about Jung's model of the psyche, along with a description of the *puer* and *senex* archetypes. According to Jung emotional states and archetypal images represent two ends of a single affect-image spectrum, and every mood state is accompanied by a corresponding archetypal image. As the human psyche generates unique archetypal images to personify various emotions, and we similarly find examples of this in ancient Greek myth where for example Eros personified love, Phobos fear, Aglos grief, Phthonus jealousy, Eudaemonia happiness, Kronos depression, Hermes mania, and so on. This model invites us to look for archetypal images appearing in the imaginations of bipolar individuals.

When it comes to personifying the forces at work in bipolar swings it is the last two of these Greek images that we will concern ourselves with – Kronos and Hermes – universal archetypal figures of myth given the more general titles of 'senex' and 'puer' by Jung.

We can begin by laying down a brief phenomenological description of the archetypes senex (representing depression) and puer (representing mania) as described by post-Jungian writer James Hillman:

The Senex Archetype

The god Saturn-Kronos is image for both positive and negative senex. His temperament is cold. Coldness can also be expressed as distance; the lonely wanderer set apart, cast out. Coldness is also cold reality, things just as they are; and yet Saturn is at the far-out edge of reality. As lord of the nethermost, he views the world from the outside, from such depths of distance that he sees it, so to speak, all upside down, yet structurally and abstractly. The concern with structure and abstraction makes him the principle of order, whether through time, or hierarchy, or exact science and system, or limits and borders, or power, or inwardness and reflection, or earth and the forms it gives.

The cold is also slow, heavy, leaden, and dry or moist, but always the coagulator through denseness, slowness, and weight expressed by the mood of sadness, depression, or melancholia. Psychologically the senex is at the core of any complex or governs any attitude when these psychological processes pass to end-phase. We expect it to correspond to biological senescence, just as many of its images: dryness, night, coldness, winter, harvest, are taken from the processes of time and of nature… It is the Saturn within the complex that makes it hard to shed, dense and slow, and maddeningly depressing –the madness of lead-poison– that feeling of the everlasting indestructibility of the complex…. We must further conclude that the negative senex is the senex split from its own puer aspect. He has lost his 'child'. [Hillman, *Puer papers*, Spring Publications 1979]

The Puer Archetype

The single archetype tends to merge the following into one: the Hero, the Divine Child, the figures of Eros, the King's Son, the Son of the Great Mother, the Psychopompos, Mercury-Hermes, Trickster, and the Messiah. In him we see a mercurial range of these 'personalities': narcissistic, inspired, effeminate, phallic, inquisitive, inventive, pensive, passive, fiery, and capricious.

The puer has a one-sided vertical direction, its Ikaros-Ganymede propensity of flying and falling. Because of this vertical direct access to the spirit, this immediacy where vision of goal and goal itself are one, winged speed, haste –even short cut– are imperative. The puer cannot do with indirection, with timing and patience. It knows little of the seasons and of waiting. And when it must rest or withdraw from the scene, then it seems to be stuck in a timeless state, innocent of the passing years, out of tune with time. Its wandering is as the spirit wanders, without attachment and not as an odyssey of experience. It wanders to spend

or to capture, and to ignite, to try its luck, but
not with the aim of going home.

Like the senex, it cannot hear, does not learn.
The puer therefore understands little of what
is gained by repetition and consistency, that is,
by work, or of the moving back and forth, left
and right, in and out, which make for subtlety
in proceeding step by step through the
labyrinthine complexity of the horizontal
world. These teachings but cripple its winged
heels, for here, from below and behind, it is
particularly vulnerable. It is anyway not meant
to walk, but to fly.

Instead of soul, of insight, the puer attitude
displays an aesthetic point of view: the world
as beautiful images or as a vast scenario. Life
becomes literature, an adventure of intellect or
science, or of religion or action, but always
unreflected and unrelated and therefore
unpsychological. It is the puer in a complex
that 'unrelates' it, that volatizes it out of the
vessel –that would act it out, call it off and
away from the psychological- and thus is the
principle that uncoagulates and disintegrates.
What is unreflected tends to become
compulsive, or greedy. The puer in any
complex gives it its drive and drivenness,
makes it move too fast, want too much, go too
far, not only because of the oral hunger and
omnipotence fantasies of the childish, but
archetypally because the world can never
satisfy the demands of the spirit or match its

beauty. Hungering for eternal experience makes one a consumer of profane events. Thus when the puer spirit falls into the public arena it hurries history along. [Hillman, *Puer papers*, Spring Publications 1979]

We can see here how senex and puer mirror the behaviors belonging to depression and mania. Jungian analyst Luigi Zoja states his belief that senex and puer mirror the same phenomenology he finds in bipolar states:

Luigi Zoja

"Senex and Puer as key concepts for interpreting a cultural situation have significance as a bi-polarity, between whose poles move the dynamics of the collective psyche. According to Jung, an archetypal demand is not pathological in itself and becomes so only when it overwhelms consciousness, be it individual or collective, and thrusts the opposite pole into unconsciousness so that the psyche suffers an imbalance and requires readjustment. In the situation I have described, the resemblance between the oscillating puer-senex movement and the manic-depressive syndrome is very marked. There is probably a correlation here between hypothesis and empirical observation, the archetypes and the clinical picture, and the connection between senex and melancholy which has already been described by several authors (Vitale, 1973). My interest lies in the meaning of the bipolarity between which these dynamics manifest themselves: ultimately life is only liveable if it is a search for equilibrium between opposing demands, for stability temporarily achieved and lost as the pendulum swings between puer and senex, mania and depression. The idea of alternation derives from Jung's concept of bipolarity and cannot really be connected with the schemata of Freud, whose sequence of phases is linear and follows a predetermined and irreversible pattern." [Zoja, L. (1987) *Analytical psychology and the Metapsychology of feeling*, Journal of Analytical Psychology, Vol 32, Number 1. pp.50-51]

Zoja elsewhere elaborates on the nature of manic states by reference to the Greek mythological figure **Icarus**, a character most often cited as an example of the puer archetype:

"A psychopathologist could see the images of the legend of **Icarus** as a description of the manic-depressive states of which every human being is a potential victim. Our moods have the right to fluctuate through the various shadings of sadness and happiness, but an excessively low or depressed emotional tenor can set up a vicious circle that cuts us off from the natural variations of our moods and leaves us imprisoned. Flying too low would have wet the feathers of Icarus' wings, forcing him to fly still lower and to wet them even further until finally finding himself engulfed by the sea; those who allow themselves too "low" a level of vitality, passively accepting all momentary set-backs, can likewise promote a condition of still greater isolation. The refusal to accept or to live up to commitments promotes a loss of self-esteem and thus still further withdrawal; the whole of the sphere of human relationships will finally collapse, and the psychic structure of the personality quickly follows suit. The warning not to fly too high is open to similar interpretation. The euphoria and hyperactivity that dominate manic states again set up a vicious circle that alters a person's sense of self-esteem, but in precisely the opposite way. If left unchecked, the fictitious sensations experienced in manic states develop into a progressive loss of contact with reality and an underestimation of risks; and the overestimation of personal capabilities exalts itself in an illusion of ever closer contact with an inexhaustible source of energy. That state of mind is nicely described by the image of flying always higher, directing oneself toward the sun. Depression as symbolized by an approach to water, and manic states as symbolized by the proximity of fire still further coincide, respectively, with

> feelings of heaviness and lightness and also to
> the physical sensations – of cold in the first
> case, and of heat in the second- that frequently
> accompany this pair of pathologies, and for
> reasons that are far more symbolic than
> environmental." [Zoja, *Growth and Guilt*,
> 1995, pp.130-131, Routledge Press].

With the phenomenology of the puer and senex now laid out we can move on to the question of management strategies for those living with bipolar disorder. Firstly we must ask what is required to interrupt the violent mood oscillations (when they exist) between mania and depression, puer and senex? There are two answers to this question; (a) medication, and (b) psychic self-management.

Medication

Yes, I'm going to go there - the dreaded M word despised by many BP individuals – and despised not without merit especially with medications too eagerly prescribed by naïve physicians that can rob an individual of legitimate and generally harmless hypomanic mood states that are frequently well managed and offer welcome relief from the leaden weight of depression. Moreover, hypomanic states frequently afford an advantage in terms of creativity and energy that non-BP individuals may rightly envy.

In working with bipolar illness it is essential to consider medications in those cases where the individual does not possess effective and sufficient management techniques demonstrated by his/her ability to regulate harmful fluctuations in mood-states - particularly in the more troubling states of extreme mania and depression, and in so-called 'mixed mood states' technically referred to as _**agitated depression**_ or _**dysphoric mania**_.

Medications are helpful in times of affective crisis, also as maintenance therapy to help reduce the recurrence of extreme or chaotic mood. There are numerous potentially beneficial medications from which to make a selection, including anticonvulsants, atypical antipsychotics, antidepressants, lithium, and more. A psychiatrist can be consulted to discuss the most suitable class of medication to help an individual gain optimal control of the worst symptoms. While many bipolar individuals are wary of mainstream medications it is this author's belief that these are a far more effective and safer option to self-medicating through chronic use of alcohol (as in the case detailed by Jung) or street drugs.

Dosage is often the key to satisfaction, necessitating a series of trials to find the lower range of medication suitable for optimising emotional stability while taking away little of the broad affective repertoire that many wish to preserve. Of the many individuals I have interviewed regarding their experience of medication's impact on energy and creativity, those on a low but stabilizing 'maintenance' dose of lithium or some other have reported the least incursion and multiple benefits – as compared with reports of diminished cognitive and side-effects with higher dosages.

The topic of non-medical management is a broad one, including such issues as emotion regulation techniques, supportive psychotherapy, social support, cognitive strategies, management of sleep patterns, diet and relationships. I do not intend to tackle these familiar topics here, as a vast self-help literature is already available online and in books, and investigative assistance of the therapy world are likewise easily sourced. The only management issue I wish touch on below is Jung's *transcendent function*, an idea offering both a goal and an archetypal orientation in the context of bipolar disorder.

The Transcendent Function

The transcendent function is described by Jung as a psychic result arising from the tension between consciousness and the unconscious factors, essentially creating a union between them. In the case of bipolar disorder the union is between the archetypes of *puer* and *senex*. Jung describes the transcendent function as follows;

> 'When there is full parity of the opposites, attested by the ego's absolute participation in both, this necessarily leads to a suspension of the will, for the will can no longer operate when every motive has an equally strong countermotive. Since life cannot tolerate a standstill, a damming up of vital energy results, and this would lead to an insupportable condition did not the tension of opposites produce a new, uniting function that transcends them. This function arises quite

naturally from the regression of libido caused by the blockage. [Ibid., par. 824.]

The tendencies of the conscious and the unconscious are the two factors that together make up the transcendent function. It is called "transcendent" because it makes the transition from one attitude to another organically possible. [*The Transcendent Function*, Collected Works Vol. 8, par. 145.]

From the activity of the unconscious there now emerges a new content, constellated by thesis and antithesis in equal measure and standing in a compensatory relation to both. It thus forms the middle ground on which the opposites can be united. If, for instance, we conceive the opposition to be sensuality versus spirituality, then the mediatory content born out of the unconscious provides a welcome means of expression for the spiritual thesis, because of its rich spiritual associations, and also for the sensual antithesis, because of its sensuous imagery. The ego, however, torn between thesis and antithesis, finds in the middle ground its own counterpart, its sole and unique means of expression, and it eagerly seizes on this in order to be delivered from its division. [*Definitions*, Collected Works Vol. 6, par. 825.]

The transcendent function is essentially an aspect of the self-regulation of the psyche. It

typically manifests symbolically and is
experienced as a new attitude toward oneself
and life. If the mediatory product remains
intact, it forms the raw material for a process
not of dissolution but of construction, in
which thesis and antithesis both play their
part. In this way it becomes a new content that
governs the whole attitude, putting an end to
the division and forcing the energy of the
opposites into a common channel. The
standstill is overcome and life can flow on
with renewed power towards new goals.
[Ibid., par. 827.]

Following the lead of Jung, Luigi Zoja reminds that
"ultimately life is only liveable if it is a search for
equilibrium between opposing demands, for stability
temporarily achieved and lost as the pendulum swings
between puer and senex, mania and depression." With
this search for equilibrium in mind we will finish here
with another quote from James Hillman entitled
'Union of Sames':

Union of Sames

With the description of the senex and puer
behind us, we now see that we have actually
been describing a secret identity of two halves
– two halves of a single archetype. This secret
identity of both faces that are actually one face
with only some differences of feature should
not astonish us, since a corresponding
feminine union of sames (the Mother-

Daughter mysteries) has been placed at the center of feminine personality.

Archetypal representations of this single figure with double aspects are: Tages, the Etruscan God who was a grey-haired boy appearing out of the furrows of a plowed field; the Islamic Chidr, a beauteous youth with a white beard; and Lao Tzu, whose name means senex-puer, ie., *"Lao" = "old" and "Tzu" = "child."* (Other literary and hagiographic descriptions of the puer-senex polarity in the same figure are given in detail by Curtus).

What might this union of sames feel like? How would it be were the polarity healed? We have only hints: some in concepts, some in images. A primary image of the union of sames is given in that "most widely cherished Renaissance maxim" *festina lente* (make haste slowly)… The dynamus of one would be combined with the order of the other. The bi-polar spirit would be ambivalent, logically incoherent but symbolically cohesive, as we see in the paradoxes of mysticism. There would be a curious intermingling of time and eternity (senex and puer), as in nature. Temporal continuity, that causal chain of history, the basis of order and the basis of ego, is broken up or broken through by the eternal. The world of Saturn is pierced through with Mercury; the silver-quick flow coagulated into solid moments: quantum jumps, spontaneous events, forgetting and foolishness, uselessness

in the world of power yet full knowledge –
"discontinuity," as Erich Neumann called it.

These are the hints of our healing. To get there
where the spirit is whole, where meaning
holds together, we have begun on a way of
mythical images. There is an advantage in
going this way towards archetypal healing, for
myth is the language of ambivalence; nothing
is only this or that; the Gods and dancers will
not stand still. [Hillman, *Puer papers*, Spring
Publications 1979]

Thematic Representation

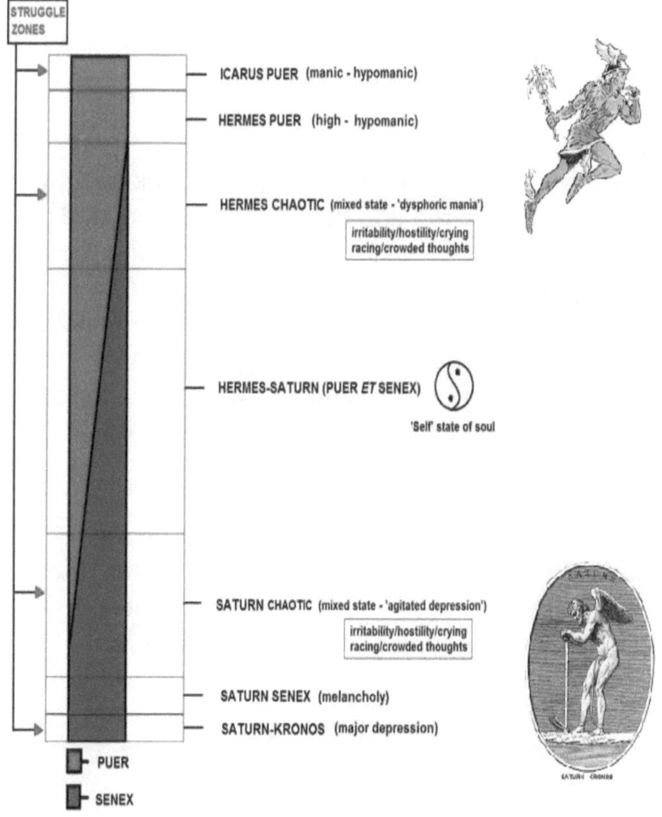

Addenda on Gender

With the typical representation of the *senex* and *puer* archetypes being Kronos and Hermes (ie. male), an exploration of Goddess figures embodying the same archetypal patterns would seem appropriate at this point. After all we live in an age of equality!

While it is difficult to locate an exact counterpart of Saturn/Kronos, the Goddess Oizys encompasses the territory of depression and many of the associated emotional states. She was the daughter of Nyx the goddess of night, and the twin of the god Momos (mockery). Her Latin name is *Miseria*, from which we derive the English word misery. Oizys is portrayed variously as the goddess of misery, anxiety, worry, grief, distress, and especially suffering, melancholy and depression.

When we come to the figure of the *puer*, Greek mythology offers an excellent female representation, namely Iris - Goddess of the rainbow and messenger of the Gods, along with her sister Arke who is sometimes affiliated with the faded second rainbow. Iris is said to travel with the speed of wind from one end of the world to the other, and into the depths of the sea and the underworld.

According to Hesiod's Theogony, Iris is daughter of Thaumas and the air nymph Electra. She is frequently mentioned as a divine messenger in the Iliad which is attributed to Homer, but does not appear in his Odyssey, where Hermes fills that role. Like Hermes, Iris carries a caduceus or winged staff. A Goddess of sea and sky, she is also represented as supplying the clouds with the water needed to refresh the world, consistent with her identification with the rainbow.

Iris is married to Morpheus the god of dreams and fantasies, or in other accounts to Zephyrus, the god of the west wind. Their son is Pothos ("Longing"). In Euripides' play Heracles, Iris appears alongside Madness, cursing Heracles with the fit of "mania" in which he kills his three sons and his wife Megara. Iris was said to have golden wings, whereas Arke her sister had iridescent ones. She is also said to travel on the rainbow while carrying messages from the gods to mortals.

Iris had numerous titles and epithets, including Chrysopteron (Golden Winged), Podas ôkea (swift footed) or Podênemos ôkea (wind-swift footed), and Thaumantias or Thaumantos (Daughter of Thaumas, Wondrous One). Under the epithet Aellopus (Αελλόπους) she was described as swift-footed like a storm-wind. She also watered the clouds with her pitcher, obtaining the water from the sea. The word iridescence is derived in part from the name of this goddess.

Footnote

For a lengthy and provocative discussion on the *union of sames,* especially as it applies to the *puer* and *senex* archetypes, read James Hillman's book **Senex and Puer (Uniform Edition)**. Throughout his works Hillman echoes Jung's contention about mythology still holding psychic relevance today, stating "The power of myth, its reality, resides precisely in its power to seize and influence psychic life. The Greeks knew this so well, and so they had no depth psychology and psychopathology such as we have. They had myths. And we have no myths as such - instead, depth psychology and psychopathology. Therefore psychology (with its 'case stories') shows myths in modern dress, and myths show our depth psychology in ancient dress."

Hillman's words will serve as a reminder to treat seriously the products of both myth and imagination, especially the imaginations of those riding the undulating waves of mania and depression. By gaining more familiarity with the imaginal figures presiding over these and other mood states we enter into a position of dialogue, and perhaps useful negotiation with the presiding powers of our lives.

References

- Hillman, J. (1979) '**Puer Papers**', Spring Publications.
- Jung, C.G., (1903) 'On Manic mood disorder' in *Psychiatric Studies* Vol-1, Collected works, second edition (1970) translated by R.F.C Hull. Routledge and Kegan Paul.

- McCurdy, J.C., (1987) 'Manic-Depressive Psychosis – A Perspective: Binswanger, Jung, Neumann, and the Myth of Dionysus' in *Journal of Analytical Psychology*, 32. pp.309-324
- Vitale, A., (1973) 'Saturn: The Transformation of the Father' in Fathers and Mothers: Five Papers on the Archetypal Background of Family Psychology, edited by Patricia Berry, pp. 5-39. Spring Publications
- Zoja, L. (1987) 'Analytical psychology and the Metapsychology of feeling': Journal of Analytical Psychology, Vol 32, Number 1. pp.47-55
- Zoja, L. (1995) 'Growth and Guilt' Routledge Press.
- Wikipedia article on the Goddess Iris.
- Theoi.com article on Iris.

www.ingramcontent.com/pod-product-compliance
Lightning Source LLC
Chambersburg PA
CBHW051407250726
48656CB00006B/2319